SEVEN PATHS TO LOVE

SEVEN PATHS
to LOVE

Pouline Middleton

New Insights
PRESS

Editor: Rick Benzel
Cover and Book Design: Susan Shankin & Associates

Published by New Insights Press
An Imprint of Over And Above Group
Los Angeles, CA
www.overandabovecreative.com

ISBN: 978-0-9965486-8-7
First edition

Printed in the United States of America

If you enjoyed reading this book, please share it with others on
Facebook, Twitter and other social media.
We'd also appreciate your review of it on Amazon or other book review websites.

CONTENTS

Introduction

Many men yearn for a life where it's okay to be in touch with their masculine identity. There are also some men who think it's hard to be the man in the home, because it is the domain of women. And then there are some men who think that there isn't enough sex in their relationship.

Many women yearn for a man they can count on, so they will not have to take care of everything themselves. Some women would like to be able to respect men more often than it happens today. And then there are some women who feel they don't get enough good sex.

If you can recognize that everyone has different needs, and you want more of yours met in the future, this part of the book presents some things you can do to get what you need. If you learn to understand these love paths and decide to follow them, you will most likely find more love, a greater sense of security in your relationship, and yes, more lovely sex.

- If you are getting ready to date someone, you can use these paths to find out if the person you meet is interesting to you.

- If you are already in a relationship, you can practice at becoming better in these areas and get the relationship that you long for, even though right now, it may seem unclear or difficult as to how to get there.

Whether you go fast or slow along these paths is not the important thing. What counts is that you follow these paths consistently and put a certain distance behind you.

Each chapter contains a detailed description of the path, and what you get out of following it. There will also be instructions on what you can do to improve your outlook. The first seven chapters (four for men and three for women) also contain instructions on what to do if you feel braver and wish to take bigger steps.

The section for the brave should be read as input on what you can do if you want to change your life's pattern. You can use these inputs to grow in your personal development process. You may often feel that the suggestions are for the very brave, but as you begin to feel familiar with the different paths, you may discover that you will want to push yourself a little further. Then it's time to read the sections *For the Brave*.

The book is divided into three parts: one for men, one for women, and one for both. That's because in some ways, there is a difference in how the genders act when we encounter love. There are also differences in how as a culture we expect women to act versus how we expect men to act when it comes to love and relationships.

Of course, there are large differences among different men, just as there are among individual women. So you might actually find it useful to read the entire book, no matter what your gender.

By the way, throughout the book, whenever I refer to your "partner," it is inclusive of any person who is your date, girlfriend, boyfriend, spouse, mate, or lover.

PART 1

Four Paths for Men

There are four paths in total that a man needs to be able to follow to be successful when it comes to love–and remember, practice makes perfect.

The four paths are:

- The-listening path
- The feeling-what's-right-for-you path
- The say-yes path
- The say-no path

The four paths are symbolic of feelings that are important to master if one wants a happy relationship.

Going down a path is a good metaphor because it signals that you move from one way of viewing and experiencing love to another, better way. You will most likely also get some extra experiences and insights while traveling.

Bon voyage!

CHAPTER 1

The Path of Listening

How to hear what's between the lines

This path is about listening to what your partner says about your life together and her expectations of you. If you don't understand what she means when she says something, anything, to you, then ask until you do.

The listening path is important because many women have opinions about you, your actions, your attitudes, and the love life you share. Whether or not you listen to her opinions about your love life, her opinions will affect it — so you might as well listen.

It can't be guaranteed that your partner is good at expressing her opinions at first. But if you continue to ask and listen to what she's saying, she will get better. She will appreciate your listening and, as a result, improve how she expresses her love to you.

You benefit from taking the listening path in two ways:

A. You get to know her concrete expectations of you in regards to your relationship.

B. Your partner will feel seen and heard and as a result her kindness and acceptance of you and your needs will grow.

How do you do it?

Whenever your partner says something about your relationship, ask her to elaborate. Maybe she will talk about how she wants you to spend more time together. Then you can ask her why and listen to the answer. You can ask her what she would like the two of you to do together. You can also suggest something yourself. Listen to her reactions and read her body language. Does she want to do what you suggest? Try to ask her if there's something you can do that makes her want to do what you want to do.

Maybe she says something about practical things at home. If she does, ask her what she's unhappy with and why. If she talks about how much work she's doing at home, listen and express your gratefulness for her big effort. If you feel you're doing your part, get a piece of paper and write down what she does, and what you do. When you have completed this list, look it over together and decide if you think the tasks are fairly (and equally) distributed.

Perhaps she mentions something about some of your tasks that haven't been completed. If she does, you can choose to admit it instantly. That shows you are listening. After, you have to decide whether or not it's realistic that you will finish them soon. Or perhaps it's better if the two of you decide together that you need to find a new deadline for the tasks at hand.

If your partner can't answer what she wants and keeps finding new obstacles to moving on lovingly, you can safely assume that she doesn't need a concrete act from you. Rather, she needs just to feel your nearness/ proximity/vicinity or love. If you listen and watch her body language, you might detect she needs an embrace or a kiss. If you give that to her, you will make her feel safe and she can then figure out if there's something you need to talk about or if the issue has been resolved, because it was more about feelings.

ADVICE NO. 1: You mustn't guess what your partner wants, but rather keep asking until you get a clear picture of what your partner's expectations are. If she's unable to answer any of your questions, ask her to think about it. Return to the issue the following evening until you understand her expectations.

For the Brave

If you are brave, you can choose to ask your partner how well she thinks your relationship is working. She will likely be surprised that you're asking. She might wonder if the reason you're asking is that you're unhappy with the relationship. Then it's great to assure her that you love her very much and that you generally think things are going well, but it would be nice if the two of you could talk about some of the smaller issues that would make you both happier if they were to get resolved better. After that you can pull out a notepad because she will likely have a list of things that could be changed for the better.

It's important at this time that you make it obvious to her that you are opening up a discussion of possible changes you are willing to make rather than trying to come to a conclusion immediately or starting to defend yourself.

The best thing would be to have this talk over the course of one or two weeks and together set a deadline for when to decide on changes you can agree upon. This is simply because it helps to make decisions on what elements you want to change in your relationship without prevarication or delay. Over the course of these days you set aside to talk about it, you can both regularly share the thoughts you're having about change, but you don't need to make decisions on everything until the deadline. Keep discussing until the deadline date you have set.

The decisions can be made the night you've set as your deadline. At that time, look over the list you each have written down or thought about and then discuss which changes are most important for you. When you have decided to go through with any changes you can agree upon, make the changes and then begin to live with the new elements.

After a couple of months, it will be beneficial to talk about how you're both finding things changed. Are there some elements that are not working as you intended them to? Are there things you decided upon that you never went through with? Is that okay? Or do you together need to do something else to go through with it? Evaluate together what you think the changes have brought in terms of results and decide if you need to make adjustments.

It's a good idea to have such a one- or two-week procedure once a year in a committed relationship. The reason it's a good idea is that we as people constantly evolve and change in small ways. We may get a new job or the children grow up a little bit more, and these changes result in different needs for us than we previously had. We may get interested in a new direction in life or want to change tracks. We may want to take a class, look for a new job, make some new friends, find a hobby, or make more time for each other.

All these and many other changes mean that the basis of your relationship and your couple's life together changes. It may not be specific big changes you can identify, but the sum of many small changes that result in a change of terms and conditions in the relationship. So it's a good idea to give your relationship a yearly checkup.

ADVICE NO. 2: Keep in mind that the terms and conditions of a romantic relationship change as we change as humans. It's a good idea to check your relationship yearly so you're certain you're both happy.

CHAPTER 2

The Path of Feeling What's Right for You

How to fully be yourself in your relationship

While you're following the listening path you might benefit from taking a stroll down the path of feeling what is right for you. How are you affected by what she says?

This path isn't as straight as the listening path was. There are four parallel tracks on the path of feeling what's right for you. They are as follow:

TRACK 1: If you feel her demands and expectations of you are fair, pay attention to the next chapter about saying yes. It means you are feeling in agreement that what she says is right for both of you.

TRACK 2: If you feel overwhelmed because she talks all the time, pay attention to the chapter about saying no. It means that you are feeling that you are not in agreement with what she says is right for both of you.

TRACK 3: If you feel that you can't currently relate to what she says but you have to think about it, tell her.

TRACK 4: If you feel you're already doing what she's asking you to do, tell her.

You will benefit in two ways from following the path of feeling what's right for you:

A. You will get better at realizing what you think is acceptable.

B. You will get better at realizing what you think is unacceptable.

How do you do it?

The path of feeling what's right for you works best if you combine it with the listening path. The reason for this is because whenever you hear something, you usually have a first reaction to what you're hearing. This reaction is incredibly important because it tells you exactly what you think is acceptable and what isn't. It reflects what you are feeling about it.

Unfortunately, many people make the mistake that they immediately share their opinion. That is rarely a good idea in a relationship. A relationship is built on the many different elements, feelings, dreams and thoughts of two different people and all these elements need to work together. If you constantly get the strong opinions of another person thrown at you, it creates an unnecessarily strong sense that the other's opinions matter more than your feelings. If you then begin throwing back your own opinions, you'll both end up talking past each other without very many openings. However, it isn't in your interest to manifest yourself so strongly because then you make disagreeing with you into a battle for who is right, rather than sharing what you are feeling.

What you have to signal to your partner is that you can tell right from wrong within yourself and you know what's important to you. But you also need to be prepared to listen so you can find out what she thinks is important. Wanting something to be different doesn't equate to things changing. You can change things only if you and your partner agree to do so. You need to take specific actions towards making changes, otherwise things are likely to stay the same.

ADVICE NO. 3: You must work on getting better at listening to what you're feeling inside, and use it to get an understanding of your inner compass. This compass is a key element for you in your relationship. And in other parts of your life.

For the Brave

If you're really brave on the path of feeling what's right for you, you'll allow yourself to feel both the feelings you're proud of and the feelings you're less proud of.

It's important to be honest with yourself about the feelings you're less proud of. It may be feelings such as stinginess, jealousy, envy or any other feeling you may have. Honesty towards yourself is important because the feelings will still be within you whether or not you're honest with yourself.

When you're dishonest with yourself about these feelings, and don't admit to them, it can result in you making the wrong decisions. That's why it's important to be honest. And we all have them. Men and women, young and old, people from every layer of society, we all have feelings we are not proud of. It's part of human nature.

And if, on a late evening, you feel really brave, you can choose to share with your partner what you're feeling. Maybe you're experiencing envy of a colleague that you think is more successful than you. Maybe you're experiencing jealousy of the neighbor because every woman, including yours, always finds him so charming.

Most women will respect you more if you're able to acknowledge your feelings. Believe it or not, your woman may already have managed to see straight through you so it will not be a big surprise to her. When you're able to put the feeling into words, it'll shrink and it won't take up as much space in your relationship, neither directly nor indirectly.

ADVICE NO. 4: There are no wrong feelings. Stand by the feelings you aren't proud of as well as the feelings you are. By doing that to yourself, you'll reduce the negative effect of the feelings you are not proud of.

CHAPTER 3

The Path of Saying Yes

How to find the key to positive intimacy

When your partner suggests something you think is fair and that you want to do, tell her clearly. Praise her for it if you think it's a good suggestion. Then do the thing you've agreed to. This last item is the most important one because if you clearly agree and then don't do it, she'll conclude that she cannot count on you.

Then you'll make her insecure and she'll begin to notice all of your mistakes and other signs telling her that you find it hard to keep an agreement. You can stop this negative development from happening by feeling what's right for you and then clearly say yes, and living up to your agreement.

Saying yes is also connected to the next chapter about saying no. A woman appreciates both answers equally, because she knows what she's dealing with when a man knows how to say yes and no in a respectful manner. She can count on her man and that makes her feel safe.

You'll benefit in two ways from following the path of saying yes:

A. Your woman will respect you more if you can properly say yes and go through with what you agree upon.

B. The more she respects you, the more she'll want to have sex.

How do you do it?

Being able to say yes requires that you've learned what it said in chapter 2 about feeling what's right for you. You have to be able to feel your own opinions and what's important in order to be able to accept a suggestion your partner makes.

It's important to stress that you don't have to say yes just because you've learned how to follow the path of saying yes. The point of this path is to train yourself to say yes when you really mean it. That's what your partner longs for: intimacy with a man who wants to be there fully.

There's nothing worse than participating in an event or an activity where the man is there only 50 percent. Then it's better for him to not participate at all because then she won't attend something with false hopes. Instead she'll go alone or invite a friend to enjoy it with.

There are often things in the joint life of a couple that you might not find very fun. It could be having to attend a family gathering with far away relatives or long lost cousins where you only know your wife or don't really care about or even like those people. It might be school events where you can't make the connection of what child belongs to which parent and which ones are your kid's friends. It can be work parties with your partner's colleagues where you have nothing to say. But that's the way it is. When you're in a committed relationship, these are things that you just have to do every now and then.

However, know that the things that you have to do are more fun if the participants decide to be there 100% instead of not really engaging and shuffling off with their faces in their phones. You don't make a good impression on the other people, who may even ask your partner "What's wrong with him?"

Another area where it's important to be able to clearly say yes are your practical duties at home. If she asks you to put up a shelf and you clearly say yes, then get it done. If it's your responsibility to mow the lawn and trim the hedges, then complete those tasks without having her remind you three or four times. What happens when she reminds you is that she loses her respect for you. She begins to view you as a boy who needs a mother to help him complete his tasks. When her respect declines, the sex drive does too.

So when you receive an invitation or a suggestion from your partner, consider whether or not you actually want to participate or complete the suggestion. If you do, say yes and get to it and actively participate. If you can't give a clear answer, you either need to ask for a little more time to find out what you think, or you can read the next chapter and learn how to say no.

ADVICE NO. 5: Register what you feel like doing or participating in, and clearly say yes to what you want to do. If you don't know what you feel about the suggestion, ask for time to think about it. When you've accepted something or you've agreed upon something, do it without complaining. When you say yes, mean it.

For the Brave

To challenge yourself, try to say yes to things you've previously said no to. It might be agreeing to change the broken window even though you've never tried to put in new windows before. It might be participating at a work party with your partner even though you're thinking it will probably be boring. Or it could be taking a class together like dancing or French, just to learn something new. Whatever you have refused to do in the past that she wanted to do, try saying yes this time.

By actively participating or completing new tasks, you may get something out of it that you hadn't expected. You might be surprised at how proud you can feel when you open and close the window you've put up yourself. Maybe you'll meet surprising guests at some relative's birthday party, or perhaps you'll talk to a guy at the work party that ends up offering you a new job or buying your services.

By doing things you aren't used to doing, you'll expand your repertoire for who you are and what you're able to do. That doesn't mean that you next time have to attend the next birthday party for the same relative, but you have the opportunity to ponder what you want to do and say yes if you want to.

ADVICE NO. 6: A big potential for your relationship development lies in doing what you aren't used to. Challenge yourself by doing at least one thing you haven't done before with your partner, and register how it makes you feel. Keep what is useful from that experience and throw the rest away.

CHAPTER 4

The Path of Saying No

How resistance can lead to more intimacy

When your wife suggests something you don't find fair or that you don't want to participate in, it is best to clearly, politely and considerately say no. To politely say no means that you're explaining to her why you don't want to do what she's asking. If you don't know whether or not you want to, go back to the chapter about the path of feeling what's right for you.

When your partner suggests a joint social activity, it's very important that you as a man clearly say yes or no. If the answer isn't clear, it's likely that she'll read some meaning into it that she thinks is what you are saying. This means that she'll take a response like "maybe" or "it's a possibility" as a tentative yes, while men often mean that they haven't decided yet but it's an option (they don't really want).

Many men believe that their partner will get angry when they turn something down. It's a possibility that she'll get disappointed that you don't want to attend her uncle's birthday party, but she'll also respect that you've considered what you want to do and are capable of saying no in a polite and considerate manner.

You'll benefit in two ways from following the path of saying no:

A. Your woman will respect you the more you can politely and considerately say no and go through with what you've said.

B. The more she respects you, the more she'll want the two of
   you to have sex.

But wait, aren't those the same two things you got out of following
the last chapter on saying yes? Indeed, they are. That is because saying
yes and saying no are closely connected. If you are only capable of one,
you won't benefit as much as when you are capable of both. Being able
to say yes and no greatly increases respect and the likelihood of having
good sex together.

How do you do it?

When your partner suggests something, the first thing you need to do is
stop and figure out what you want to do. She might be adding another
task to a list you already think is too long. Then explain to her that you
realize there's a need for the task to be completed, but there's no room on
the list for another thing right now. You can also suggest that she prioritize the tasks so you'll begin with the one that's most important to her, or
that you will prioritize the list together

In the perfect world, everything is running smoothly all by itself, but
it's rarely like that in a relationship. If the two of you after a couple of
conversations can't figure out what different tasks need to be done, or
how often they need to be done, it's either because your demands are too
high or you have very different opinions about the tasks.

In a relationship, you have to compromise on a lot of things. If you
can't live with the level of effort your partner puts into keeping up a
specific part of your household, you might need to take responsibility for
the thing you are unhappy with and do it yourself as often as you find it
necessary.

Another possibility is that she invites you to an event with some of
her friends whom you find boring. Then explain to her that you think
they're boring and therefore you only want to attend every fourth time
they invite you to something.

Or maybe you need a weekend away with the boys or just time to
look into the bonfire without speaking. If so, make it clear to her that this

is important to you. You can also ask her if she wants to have a spa day or go hiking with a friend or maybe go to a party by herself.

If she keeps begging to do something you've said no to, go back to the listening path and work on your ability to listen to why it's so important to her. Then follow the path of feeling and choose whether or not you want to say yes or no. Remember that women don't expect to get their way with everything. Some women can be stubborn and insist that something needs to be done. But stick to your own opinion, if it's important to you that you don't do it.

A smart woman will then respect you more because she can feel that you hold onto who you are and your own masculinity. When she can sense your limits and that she can't trick you, she'll feel safe with you. The more politely and considerably you say no, the more she'll respect you.

ADVICE NO. 7: Find the courage to say no in a proper manner. Stick to what you think even when you are faced with resistance. And remember that sometimes a warm hug can thaw an icy facade.

For the Brave

This path is the hardest one for most men to follow because here you need to hold onto what's important to you even though it isn't popular. A number of men feel bad if their woman gets angry. They will actually go to quite some length to avoid it. But it is important to be able to handle her anger if you want her to feel safe with you and to respect you. To find this courage is the key to more intimacy and good sex.

Yes, this is a simplification of what's happening between men and women but since I experience that women want men who can say no in a polite and considerate manner, and men want more space to say no, I think it can work much better than how it works today if you as a man train your capacity to follow this fourth path.

The brave man finds his direction in life and takes initiative to follow it. This means he sets goals and he sticks to them even though they aren't always popular. When the man knows what he wants and actively does something to reach those goals, the woman can feel him as a person and support his direction and progress. That makes her respect him more.

A man who can tell his partner that right now he needs to focus on (fill in the blank) creates respect. If he's also capable of focusing his attention on her in a lovingly focused way, every so often, she'll feel special and loved. A tip for men about this is that many women need attention often but no woman needs him to be there all the time so he loses contact with what's important to him. Then she loses respect for him.

ADVICE NO. 8: Focus on your partner every so often, like you do with your hobbies or being with your good friend. When you're being focused on by your loved one, you feel loved.

PART 2

Three Paths for Women

There are three paths that a woman needs to be able to follow confidently to succeed in love — and remember, practice makes perfect!

The three paths are:

- The path of finding pride
- The path of feeling what's right for you
- The path of letting go

These three paths are symbolic of feelings that are important to master if one wants a happy relationship.

The path is a good metaphor because it signals that you move from one way of viewing and experiencing love to another and better way of viewing and experiencing love. You will most likely also get some extra experiences and insights while travelling.

Bon voyage!

CHAPTER 5

The Path of Finding Pride

How to find peace in an imperfect body

It's important for you to feel proud of your body and your femininity because it'll bring you daily happiness and give you energy. This is not to say that your mind does not count and that beauty trumps intelligence. I am not saying that. Your partner is with you, hopefully as much for your mind as for your body, but I know that most women struggle with body image, and it impacts their confidence about their mind.

On this path, we'll work on this skill because so many women look at their bodies and do not feel pride. Maybe it'll begin with feeling proud with just parts of your body. That will then expand and become more and more parts, and in the end you might feel proud of your whole body and your femininity.

A woman who can find multiple things about herself and her body that she's proud of is able to not only be happy herself, but also be happy for her man by flaunting it. To focus on what you're proud of is a contributing factor in creating a positive spiral where happiness and surplus energy in a relationship is boosted.

You'll benefit in two ways from following the path of finding pride:

A. You'll experience being happier with life, the prouder you are about all or parts of your body.

B. You'll experience positive energy by focusing on everything about yourself that makes you happy.

How do you do it?

You start by finding what you like most about your body. Is it your hands? Or the way your shoulder is arched? Or the shape of your ankle? Get a piece of paper and write down all the things about your body that you like. If you come across a part of your body that you don't like, just ignore it and keep focusing on the positive.

In the following days and weeks, you have to focus on these elements when you look at yourself in the mirror, when you see your reflection in a shop window or when your partner or a random man pays you a compliment. Enjoy that these elements of your body exist and that you like them.

The more areas you can find, the better. And nothing is too small. Maybe you think the nail on your little finger is beautiful or your hair just after you've washed it. Enjoy every element you can feel happiness about. And keep ignoring the elements that bother you.

ADVICE NO. 9: Focus on what you like about your body and ignore the rest.

For the Brave

Tell yourself that you're beautiful no matter how your body looks. Those extra pounds don't matter. The inches you're lacking aren't in fact lacking. The breast measurement you long for isn't worth the longing.

By deciding that you're great as you are, you become great. When you don't have to worry about everything that is wrong, and instead focus on what makes you happy, you're making space for powers previously tied down by worries. And since you can't worry your way out of a problem, and worrying only creates more worry, you're better off not thinking about it. Simply decide to let go of worries about yourself and your looks.

At first after you've made this decision, the old worries will still come flooding, but as you're moving further along the path of finding pride where you won't allow space for worries, the happier you will become. You will also become stronger because a mind without worry stands stronger when faced with challenges than a mind heavy with worry. And remember, worries aren't useful for anything.

As you clear your mind of worries about your body, you'll most likely experience that you feel like having more sex. You will no longer, during the act, look at a lump of fat you wish wasn't there but rather look at the beautiful curve of your buttock. You will feel increased enjoyment because accept of your body as it is makes it possible for you to be present. Being present and the feeling of enjoyment are closely connected.

It's brave of you to accept your whole body as it is because we live in a society where women are constantly presented with pictures of the perfect female body. But remember that even the more beautiful models get Photoshopped, where wrinkles freckles, pimples, and saggy skin that doesn't fold right is removed before we see the pictures. No one, absolutely no one, looks the way they do in the magazines, so why should an artificial body image affect your perception of yourself and thereby your enjoyment?

If you want to be even more brave, then go to the pool or the beach and force your thoughts to only focus on what makes you happy about your body. It takes 21 days to change a habit if you make an active effort every day. You can begin today if you want to.

ADVICE NO. 10: Decide that you no longer want to worry about yourself and your looks, because a mind without worry stands stronger when faced with challenges.

ADVICE NO. 11: Use your body to feel how being present and feeling enjoyment is closely connected.

ADVICE NO. 12: Every time you say that you hate something about your body, you have to mention two things that you love to balance out the negative/positive energy.

CHAPTER 6

The Path of Feeling What's Right for You

How vulnerability can be a strength

This path of feeling what's right for you is the only path men and women have in common. This path is the direct path to intimacy. When you both feel what you like and don't like, and when you feel there's room for your opinion, the possibility of intimacy between you two grows.

The path of feeling what's right for you isn't as straight as the path of finding pride. For women, it's a wider path with three tracks:

TRACK 1: Working on your ability to show and accept vulnerability.

TRACK 2: Being confident with your own sexual wants and needs.

TRACK 3: Separating things out and telling things apart.

Feeling what's right for you and expressing it in a considerate manner gives direct access to intimacy. When you're good at recognizing what feels right and what doesn't feel right for you, it's much easier to say yes and no. When you can't recognize what feels right or wrong or don't have the courage to say it, but maybe rather focus on what other people think or the expectations they have of you, then you continue to live with a distance to intimacy.

You'll benefit in three ways from following the path of feeling what's right for you:

A. You'll find your inner compass and figure out how to keep using it.

B. You'll be in better control of your (love) life.

C. You increase the likeliness of intimacy in a relationship.

How do you do it?

It's important that you make an effort to follow all three tracks. Many women know what they feel but find it hard to express it in a way so it'll be respected or to stand their ground when faced with resistance from their partner.

Working on the ability to show and accept vulnerability

You may need to force yourself to feel how what your partner says or does affects you when working on the ability to accept your feminine vulnerability. When you've felt that you need to sort through it all and identify which are the important and which are the less important things, you can begin to understand your areas of vulnerability.

It's often a good idea to keep a journal for a couple of weeks where you write something on the positive list every time your partner does something you like and then put 1 to 5 stars by the line. One star shows it was okay and five stars shows it was completely amazing.

Do the same thing with the negative list. Write things down and score them by how much it crossed your line of acceptability. One star shows it was only a little over the line, and five stars shows it was way past the line.

After a couple of weeks, use this journal to make yourself a status report. You do this by making a list based on the elements that are on the positive and negative list. You also put them into groups correlated to how many stars they've gotten. And then try to recognize the patterns and what the two lists say. How many 1 star items are there? 5 star? See if you can decipher its meaning in terms of how often your partner helped you feel good versus how often your partner crossed the line a lot with you. Then tell your partner about your list and what it says.

The man will likely be surprised by some of the points. Maybe you got surprised too. But no matter if it's a surprise or maybe a bit of embarrassment over how sensitive you are, when it comes to specific topics, you've just drawn up an image of your inner vulnerability compass.

You need to use this inner compass in the future to ensure that you receive more intimacy from your partner and less flack. You can distinguish the areas where you are comfortably vulnerable versus uncomfortably vulnerable.

The inner compass is the tool that makes a woman capable of feeling her vulnerability and articulating when her boundaries are being overstepped. This creates a basis for clear communication and boosts the man's respect for the woman. If it doesn't, you need to find a man with whom it does.

ADVICE NO. 13: Prioritize feeling where your boundaries are and letting your partner know. Clear boundaries create a good environment for the respect among partners. Respect is the basis for intimacy with one's partner in a healthy relationship.

Being confident with sexual wants and needs

Some women are in close contact with their own sexuality but a lot of women aren't. This is partly due to the fact that we, in our culture, have very few positive words for a horny female who enjoys sex and that we as a culture look down upon women who do what they want when it comes to sex. Interestingly enough, there are many positive words for a horny male and we often express forbearance when he does what he wants when it comes to sex, almost like we expect it of him.

There are very few positive words for a horny woman, if any. When the culture is so bad at giving a woman a deep feeling of pride over her own sexuality, a woman has to get it herself: she needs to find out what turns her on and then ask her partner for more of exactly that.

What do you do if you don't really know what turns you on? Well, then you're a member of a large club of women because there are a lot of women who feel like that. Then you need to choose between whether it will continue like that or whether you might start on a small journey in and around your own desire to find out what turns you on.

Here are a couple of the steps to find out what turns you on:

- You can purchase a porn magazine and look at different sexual situations. Some of them will turn you on, others not at all.

- You can go on the internet on redtube.com or other porn sites and all by yourself look through some porn clips. Here you'll probably also find clips that turn you on and others that absolutely don't.

- You can go to a sex shop, either online where you can see and read about quite a bit of equipment, or into a bricks and mortar sex store where you can touch things, too. Both are good for showing which elements in sexual play turn you on and that you can try discovering further. You may have to return to such a store a couple of times, since it can be quite overwhelming the first time you go.

- You can buy some sex toys to try them. First alone and then with your partner.

- You can do whatever spurs your curiosity in terms of getting to know the barriers between you and better sex.

It's important for women to have a sexual space that's only theirs, which means a mental space where the man doesn't automatically have access. Here, she can have fantasies that she's ashamed of or doesn't want to live out but that still turn her on. She can also have sex toys that she uses to explore her own sexuality. And if she then one day feels ready, she can bring the fantasies and the toys into the shared space.

To take responsibility for a woman's sexuality and how it's acted out lies 100% with the woman. It's a very important step to take for the individual woman. Because if she doesn't feel good about her own sexuality it's very difficult to get a well-functioning sex life with a man that can continue to be well-functioning for years and years.

And not having a well-functioning sex life affects every aspect of your joint life. When the intimacy gets smaller, the issues get bigger. The impotence and coldness can grow, and at some point, one or the other will meet another person who seems like they are more capable of fulfilling the partner's sexual wants and needs.

The more a woman knows her own needs and wants, the better she's able to guide the man in the direction that satisfies her and the more she'll want to satisfy him, too. The better both persons know themselves, the bigger the possible lane will get. No matter your age, it's never too late to start exploring your own and the other person's desire.

A note about worries here too: If you are worried about whether your partner is satisfied with his sex life with you, have a look at how often you have sex and if you're having good sex. Be honest with yourself. Do you think his needs are being met?

If he has a low sex drive and you do too, it's completely fine. But if you have different sex drives, there's a risk one of you isn't satisfied. If it's your partner who isn't satisfied, one of two things can happen:

A. He'll shrink and lose his energy and excitement about life and you'll slowly lose respect for him.

B. He'll go out and find a woman who desires him and is willing to provide him with the sex life he fantasizes about.

Remember that you, as the woman, have as much of the opportunity and responsibility as you want to take initiative for your sex life to make it more active and satisfying, which you will both benefit from.

ADVICE NO. 14: Decide to get to know your own sexuality. And enjoy the wonderful hours you'll have by getting to know your own sexuality better.

Telling things apart

It's important to be able to tell your feelings apart so you can always figure out what's bothering you. If you don't, there's a risk you'll complain about one thing when in fact it's another thing that's bothering you.

When it comes to issues that bother you or disrupt the relationship that you cannot articulate precisely, it's often an indication of intimacy lacking between you and your partner. Not being able to put your finger on what's bothering you can show itself by your feeling he's taking you for granted or he's not mentally present — or that you don't spend enough time together.

When he then walks away from the dinner table without clearing it even though that was the deal, you can get infuriated. But if you get much angrier than is reasonable for a dirty plate, a glass and some cutlery, it means something else is happening. Without being able to separate it out and telling things apart, you make it difficult for him to understand what's wrong. He'll often feel something else is the matter but he won't know what.

You have to work on your ability to figure out what's wrong and get infuriated because of that, and then ignore the dirty plate and cutlery.

ADVICE NO. 15: The better you get at telling things apart and reacting to exactly what's bothering you, the more you'll increase the chance of intimacy between you and your partner.

For the Brave

The brave woman shows her man that she's vulnerable. She can do that by talking about her vulnerability in a specific situation. Or by showing her vulnerability when you're intimate together. It can be showing vulnerability about something you've been invited to or a big home project you're about to start. It can also be about a new sexual thing you're trying out together. By showing your vulnerability every now and then, you give him the chance to take care of you and protect you.

A lot of men enjoy playing that part and can experience feeling even more closely connected to their partner. Are you aware, for example, that a man can get an erect penis by caring for his woman when she feels vulnerable? That happens because he feels that she needs him and he can be there for her. Allow yourself to enjoy that.

For most couples, it'll be important to have sex regularly if they want the love to last. In our culture it has been true for centuries that men take the initiative when it came to sex and women hold back so things don't go too far. It's still often like that in many relationships, despite the fact that they are supposed to be equal sexual partners.

If you both want to, you can choose to discuss and agree upon who will take most of the initiative in your sexual relationship. For instance, you can choose to watch porn together, taking turns who chooses the films. Or you can choose to take turns in initiating the time of day to have sex if each of you has different preferences.

Another option is that together you explore what new kinds of sex you want to have (with the possibility of saying no thank you if what is being suggested doesn't turn you on at all.) For example, you might go to a sex shop together with your husband, or to a sex fair or a swinger club together if that turns you on.

You might also try one or more of the sexual activities that don't immediately turn you on. This has to be done in a safe space with a man who understands how to respect your boundaries. If you do it together, it can lead to an expansion of your sexual repertoire. And sometimes you will be surprised by your own sexual desires, too.

ADVICE NO. 16: Try something you haven't tried before and share your insecurities and vulnerability with your partner while you're exploring what's new. Your man will enjoy being there for you and with you.

CHAPTER 7

The Path of Letting Go

How you can get everything you want as
long as you don't want everything.

Since the 1960s, women have had a lot of new possibilities open up to them. For the majority of these possibilities, women today have been in the forefront of exploring them. This means that you can't really get advice about how to get the most out of these opportunities. No one has gone before you to learn from mistakes and offer you advice. Often women will also experience a sense that there are so many opportunities, there's a risk you might drown in them, especially when you want everything.

Many women are turned on by responsible men. This is because most women have a 360-degree attention span that provides them with insight into how many things actually need to get done to have a fully functioning daily life. There are many tasks that need attention and many details that need to be in order for humans to thrive.

If a woman feels all alone having to take this responsibility, she gets tired and the love for her partner withers. Men don't need to take on every responsibility, far from it, but the woman needs to experience that he accepts his part of the joint responsibility. When a man is responsible, the woman will feel her safety grow and then she'll want to have sex with him and share her love.

However, let's face it. Not all men have learned how to take responsibility for themselves and their family. When the masculinity is absent, and the woman finds it difficult to choose between her many activities in her life, the risk of having a breakdown increases. It's simply too hard to pick and choose between priorities and possibilities and be all alone handling the whole thing.

To make sure this doesn't happen, you need to follow the path of letting go.

You'll benefit in two ways from following the path of letting go:

A. You'll learn to enjoy life.

B. You'll experience a boost in intimacy.

How do you do it?

Brew a cup of tea or coffee and get comfortable with a notebook and a pen or your computer. When you've had a sip, begin to make a list of all your daily responsibilities, divided into two separate lists. The first covers your responsibilities at work, the second covers your responsibilities at home.

When you've completed the lists, look them over and ask yourself if it's fair that you are responsible for so many things. Is it more than your partner has to handle, as far as you know? If it isn't, there's no problem. But if you realize that more and more tasks have been added to your list without you actually agreeing to being responsible for those things, then it's time to work with the two lists.

First you have a look at the list of work-related responsibilities. Read through the list and then prioritize: What are the three most important areas? And the next three? And the next three?

Maybe you'll remember a couple more things that you're also responsible for. If you do, put them on the list. Then look at the list and decide that in the future you only want to be responsible for the first nine points. The rest you can delegate to other people or simply ignore. It might have some consequences if you choose to ignore some responsibilities, but if you've been good at prioritizing your responsibilities to the top nine, it's likely that the ones further down on the list aren't actually all that important. Nine priorities are already a lot to handle.

If you think it's unfair to ignore some of your responsibilities, then try to take a look at your male colleagues at work. In the vast majority of cases, you'll see that they are already prioritizing like this. Maybe they're even down to six areas of responsibility.

Do the same with your responsibilities at home. Here it's more important to distribute some of the important responsibilities to your partner and maybe children. The more you distribute the important responsibilities, the more it'll create a feeling of a closely knit family because everybody is helping to make the family work as a unit.

The path of letting go is supposed to teach you to let go of what isn't as important simply because no human has the energy to make everything that needs to happen, happen. If you constantly have unfinished responsibilities, the risk that you'll never get to the point where you can enjoy life is very big.

You're also sacrificing intimacy because your family will rarely experience that you're being present if you're constantly worried about the responsibilities and tasks you have remaining to do. Then they'll go look for intimacy elsewhere and you might end up feeling lonely.

But don't cry about it; it's easy to do something about it and get intimacy back. Begin by making the list and let go of what isn't important.

Advice no. 17: You aren't obligated to take on every single responsibility around you. You have the right to prioritize the important and ignore the rest.

For the Brave

The brave can choose to make one more list in addition to the other two. At the top they'll write: I have about 85 years here on earth and if I were able to freely pick and choose, how would I like my life to be?

Then you have to be brave enough to be completely honest with yourself. What means something? Which situations do you remember long after they happened because they went straight to your heart? What kind of intimacy do you long for? What kind of life do you want? What kind of love life do you want?

Write it all down and maybe use a couple of days to think it through and feel what's right for you.

When you've defined what it is you want more of, make a plan for how to get it and make it happen.

ADVICE NO. 18: Decide that you no longer want to live your love life as if it's a draft of your real life. This is your real love life now, and the sooner you define what you specifically want out of it, the sooner you get to live like that.

PART 3

Three Paths that Lead Away from Love

The first seven chapters have been focused on what men and women need to do to get more intimacy and love with their partner. The next three chapters focus on some of the things you might already be doing or that you risk doing that pull you in the wrong direction. This is the direction that leads you to feeling lonely because you've pushed your partner away. Or where you can feel so misunderstood that you believe not even your partner really understands you.

Maybe you've entered a downward spiral that you can't really escape from. What follows are some tools you can use when you want to stop doing activities and taking actions that keep you away from intimacy and love in your life.

These three "side" paths are for both men and women. You can work on moving away completely from the first two paths whether you have a partner or you are single. The third path is most relevant when you're already in a relationship.

The three side paths are unfortunately a lot stronger in attracting people to follow them than the seven paths because negative energies easily drown out the positive. To learn to control and limit the negative energies in your life, it's important to take avoiding these three side paths seriously. As soon as you begin following one of them, it's easy to just keep walking, thinking you are going the right way. It can be very difficult to convince yourself to turn around. It's a lot easier just not heading down these side paths at all.

CHAPTER 8

The Path of Complaining

When a person is unhappy, he or she will likely complain. Sometimes the purpose of complaining is to change what they're unhappy about. But often it's just about complaining.

You can complain about your phone subscription and the fact that it is completely impossible to understand the terms and conditions of it. You can complain about the food available in the cafeteria. You can complain about the weather. You can complain about the cost of a movie ticket or how many people were in line at the supermarket. A certain amount of complaining is human. This isn't the kind of complaining I'm referring to on the side path of complaining.

This path is about the kind of complaining that begins when you meet a person. You open your mouth and out drop complaints about your partner's behavior and all of his or her mistakes. Complaints over all kinds of things in your relationship, small or big, old or new. You fill the common space with unsatisfied wailing—and that's all you really have to say.

Your friends, acquaintances, co-workers, and even your partner will little by little get tired of listening to you. After a certain amount of complaining, the other person leaves. The time between phone calls gets longer and longer and new meetups no longer get planned. At the end, you just stop being in touch.

If you're the one complaining, you might not understand why your relationship isn't working, or why your contacts turn into strangers and why new meetings don't turn into new friendships or new romantic relationships.

The challenge is often that you can't hear yourself. You complain, complain, complain without seeing how your words turn everything bad around you. Your complaining becomes toxic to others.

Complaining is rarely an active choice, it's just something that happens. You were unhappy with something and then you got unhappy with another thing and life is full of things to get frustrated with. And even though you complained about what you were unhappy with to begin with, it didn't change anything. Complaining isn't the way to solve issues.

Interestingly enough, your partner or friends rarely tell you or ask you to stop complaining. And if they do, it's not guaranteed that you can hear they're right. So you keep complaining and eventually your partner will start to move away from you and seek new people to talk to. So your relationship withers and your circle of friends gets smaller. And smaller. And smaller.

How do you avoid this side path?

If you want to stop complaining, you need to find the core of what makes you unsatisfied.

Maybe you find it difficult to acknowledge that you feel lonely. Or that you miss intimacy with another. Maybe you've regretted some of the things you've done, or the way your life has turned out. Perhaps you are unhappy about how you've treated others, but you find it difficult to consider finding those you've mistreated and fix what you messed up. Instead you complain. By doing that, you're in a downward spiral that leads to more loneliness that slowly can turn into bitterness.

If you want to change this behavior, you first need to ask yourself if you're ready to see a side of yourself that you probably don't like? Can you look at your own dark side, your own Shadow?

If you can answer yes, buy a notebook dedicated to this topic. It can be a cheap one, or an expensive one as you please since you're the only one who needs to use it. Put this notebook somewhere central where you can see it at all times. Every time you open your mouth during a day, write down three to five words about what you were talking about.

If you experience that you opened your mouth to complain, you have to write in greater detail what you were complaining about.

After a week, count together how many times you've complained. If it's more than a couple of times a day, or if you haven't spoken about anything other than things you're unsatisfied with, it's time to clean up your act.

Then ask three to five people who know you well if they think you complain too much. Ask them to be honest. And if they say that they do think you complain too much, ask them how that affects your friendship, relationship or family life.

Write down what they say to you in the notebook. Then look at your diary of complaining and what the people closest to you have said. Can you recognize what it says?

Make a cup of tea or coffee, maybe get a piece of cake or a biscuit and get comfortable. Now you need to feel what you're so unsatisfied with in your life, that you need to fill it with so much complaining.

Is it your joint life with your mate that isn't working? If you are single, do you miss having a boyfriend / girlfriend? Do you experience that you're lacking intimacy? Do you feel lonely? Do you feel that your family isn't the one you once dreamed about? Do you feel disappointed in life and what it has had to offer you? Nothing is too small and nothing is too big to examine.

Maybe you'll experience that it's difficult for you to find out what's underneath your complaining. If that's the case, you might need to book a couple of hours with a coach or a therapist. These are people who are educated to help you get through the shields we build to not feel a certain pain. If you have a close friend who wants the best for you, and in whom you have complete trust, it might also be possible to talk it through with him or her.

The main thing here is that these shields need to be broken down for you to be able to get out of a life clouded with complaints.

When you, by yourself or with the help of others, have found out what makes you unsatisfied, it's time to decide if you want to make an effort to change it. If you want to, you need to use a couple weeks, or a month to figure out what you want to do. What is it you need to change so you'll get more of what you long for?

Every time you begin complaining, you need to stop and go back to your plans concerning how you can get more of what you long for.

ADVICE NO. 19: Use your habit of complaining as a reminder that instead of complaining, you need to do something positive to make your dreams become a reality.

For the Brave

There's nothing in particular for the brave to do here, because it is already really, really brave to explore and feel what you're longing for and to decide that you want to actively do something to get more of it.

CHAPTER 9

The Path of Blaming Others

This side path is somewhat related to the side path of complaining. Maybe one of the things you're doing when complaining is blaming others for the life you're living.

It's a very human thing that we want where we are in life to be the fault of someone else. Maybe we had a difficult childhood, or we had a bad teacher in the first years of our school life. Perhaps one sibling got everything and you never got anything. Or you think your mother liked your brother better. Maybe you have a feeling that you're always unlucky while your neighbor is the lucky guy.

All of those are examples on how we often explain to ourselves that where we are is not our responsibility. It was someone else's fault that we did not get what we deserve.

Let me change your view of blame. It's very possible that you had a difficult childhood or a bad teacher. It's also possible that your sibling always got it all and your mother liked your brother better and maybe the neighbor is eternally lucky.

The problem is, it's pathetic to listen to a person who keeps feeling sorry for himself or herself. Especially if it's because of things that happened years ago.

In the old times, there was a grieving period after a loved one had passed away. For a year you'd dress in all black and people would take the fact that you were grieving into account. When the year was over, you'd begin wearing regular clothes again and once again participate alongside everybody else.

You should think about that when something drastic happens to you. If you, after a year, still complain about something that happened in your life, you're making what happened a condition of living. If you've been diagnosed with a serious disease that you won't die of but have to live with, and you can't think about anything else, you have to be attentive to the fact that you're creating a space around you where your illness is always in focus.

By doing that, you're making it really difficult for yourself to keep growing as a person. You're also making it difficult for the people closest to you to keep being in your life. Because they have to accept your blaming, and watch you make your life focus on this illness, that awful childhood, some jealousy of a sibling, some lucky neighbor or whatever else it might be.

What do you do to avoid this side path?

It can provoke anxiety to begin avoiding this side path because it means you have to become aware of what kind of story you're telling about yourself. Are you ready for that?

So get yourself your notebook or your iPad and begin writing down what kind of story you're constantly telling about yourself. If you can't figure out what kind of story you're telling about yourself, place the book somewhere accessible and write down every time you notice something you're saying about yourself and the story or explanation you give others for why something is the way it is in your life.

You might also sit down and begin to describe your life in your notebook. How did it begin, what happened back then, and so on and so forth? When you've written this story, put it away for a day or two. Pull it out again and look at what you've written.

- Are there any explanations on why you are where you are?
- Do you feel mostly lucky? Or unlucky?
- Who is responsible for your life being the way it has been so far?

Try to see if you can find a pattern in the explanations you give yourself and others.

When you've had a look at your story, now is the time to be honest with yourself and see if you're responsible for how your life has been ... or if other people are really the ones responsible.

Then get a glass of soda or a stiff drink and get comfortable. Now you need to consider if you want other people to be responsible for your life in the future too. If you do, then you are exactly where you're supposed to be in life. Others were responsible for your life in the past, and others will continue to be responsible in the future. Does that sound like much of a life?

If you don't want other people to be responsible for your life, you need to say goodbye to this explanation. Maybe you need to rewrite your story again but with all the details this time. Details about your awful childhood, your bad teacher, your annoying siblings, your stupid neighbor or whomever else might have ruined your life up until now. Then put the story in a drawer and say goodbye. Or even better, burn it in the fireplace or arrange a ceremonial burning some safe place in nature, on a beach for example, where there is no chance you'd cause a forest fire that you'd be responsible for.

When you've done this, you'll likely experience something of a void that can cause stomachaches for most people. But don't give up, because now is the time to fill this void with new explanations about who you are and where you'd like to go when you take responsibility for your own life.

And remember, the reason you're leaving the story about yourself as a victim is because very few people can stand listening to a person who feels sorry for themselves. By letting go of the victim story, you're making room for action and doing things your own way, so when you meet a new person, the new person can feel you and who you are today rather than listening to a victim story that you can't change anyway.

ADVICE NO. 20: To get a dignified love life where you can fulfill some of your longings, you need to take responsibility for what you do and the results your actions create.

For the Brave

There's nothing in particular for the brave to do here, because deciding that you no longer want to follow this side path of blame, and take concrete steps away every time you find yourself on this side path is brave in itself.

CHAPTER 10

The Path of Drawing the Sex Card

This last side path is one you need to avoid following when you're in a committed relationship, whether you're married or not.

Drawing the sex card means that for different reasons you use sex as a reward or punishment. Both are equally bad.

When you get an invitation to have sex because your partner begins caressing or kissing you, or both, you need to feel whether or not you want to have sex. If you do, then caress and kiss back.

If you don't want to have sex, you need to ask yourself why. Is it because you're tired? Or did you have sex not too long ago so your desire has been met? Then you say that and your partner respects it.

However, if you've lost the drive because your partner didn't clean up after dinner, came home late without calling or wasn't mentally present when watching TV together, or... (fill in the blank) and you didn't tell him how much it bothered you when it happened, and now the frustration is still taking up space within you so much in fact that he/she is not going to get any sex, then you've gotten onto the side path that's called drawing the sex card.

Another kind of drawing the sex card is partly drawing the sex card. A possibility is that you know your partner loves a specific kind of sex that you consciously deny to do to punish for something that happened outside of bed. That's just as stupid as drawing the sex card.

Making sex a reward or punishment drags you away from your desire and into the area where you're keeping score. You begin keeping an eye on what the other takes part in, how much they contribute, and then you begin giving rewards and punishments in the form of intimate moments. This destroys love.

Maybe it doesn't feel like a side path, but rather a practical way of making things stay the way you like them to be. What you often overlook is that you can't draw the sex card without consequences. Your partner feels rejected and maybe doesn't understand why. Your partner experiences that you're being aggressive when there's no good explanation for it. That makes your partner feel unsafe. When you draw the sex card, it takes the intimacy out of the intimate space.

Removing the intimacy from the intimate space is the first step down the spiral of "discussions, fights, and separation" and that can end in divorce. Drawing the sex card as a reward or punishment can never lead to more intimacy, so that must be avoided at any cost.

What do you do to avoid this side path?

You have to be attentive to when your loved one does something that annoys you, and then you have to practice your ability to react to it as soon as possible. That is the time to address the issue together, not when you get in bed.

You have to decide that no matter what comes between you and your partner, you'll never punish or reward with sex. You can talk to your partner about it and together you can agree that if one or the other draws the sex card, you must make each other aware of it.

If you aren't aware whether or not you've drawn the sex card, you can ask your partner. If the partner doesn't know either, there's not a problem. But often the partner is very aware of it.

When you choose not to draw the sex card, you'll experience, little by little, a more harmonic daily life. This happens because you're getting better and better at clearing misunderstandings and issues because there's no longer a place to punish them.

ADVICE NO. 21: Decide to get over what happened when it happened, so you can both concentrate on enjoying each other instead of punishing one another.

Epilogue

You've now read about the seven paths to follow, and the three side paths to avoid, to reach love. The purpose of being aware of these paths is that seven of them lead to more intimacy and love, and three of them lead away from intimacy and love.

It's the quality of our emotional connections to our partner and other people we're close to that determines how happy we are in life and how well we thrive, so it's a really good idea to do something to secure the intimacy. The paths in this book are tools to give you more of the intimacy in the way you want it.

Intimacy isn't just intimacy. To make partners feel close, it has to be intimacy in exactly the way you enjoy it. It's important to be able to feel when things are moving in the wrong direction and to say something about it while there's still time. It's also important to be able to feel which direction you want it to go and to affect the time together so it moves in that direction.

Keep in mind that every relationship is made up by different needs for intimacy and those needs can change over the course of a week, a month, or a year. This means that you need to have a well-developed sense of your own needs and boundaries and of your partner's needs and boundaries, respecting the fact that they can change.

The more you strengthen your own base and get good at saying yes and no to the other in a considerate manner, the more intimacy you'll experience. This is only applicable if both partners in a relationship are interested in taking responsibility for their own needs and boundaries.

If only one partner says yes or no politely, it'll be difficult to create the respect that over time strengthens the intimacy.

A love contract?

It's also important that both the man and the woman are attentive to whether the relationship balance is being upheld. How the many areas of the relationship are working and which areas that are important to one of you are failing — all can be found out by talking often about how you're both doing. It's also a good idea to talk about the relationship in a very focused way once a year.

Some couples wish to formalize their agreement in a "love contract." Such a contract was nicely defined in a Danish book by Sara Skaarup, *Kærlighedskontrakten,* which is not yet available in English but will be soon. You write down how you want to live together and which values you agree should dominate the relationship. Perhaps honesty is important to you both, or a shared attitude about how you will always try to resolve conflicts. Another issue to spell out is how you will deal with it if one of you is very jealous. Both partners need to be aware of this when going to a party together, as an example, so the contract can spell out the rules.

The love contract has two parts: one main part with general principles of your relationship, and one smaller part more focused on daily life, tasks, and chores. A possibility is that you agree on how to divide tasks at home, or to participate in family activities with the in-laws or who has the primary contact with the school. All of these things affect your daily life and are possible to get into fights about if you haven't agreed upon who's doing what.

You don't have to make it formal with an actual contract that you sign. The most important thing is that every now and then you talk about how you're both doing and that you are willing to change things that aren't going well. The challenge is that if you aren't doing that well, it can be the beginning of a downwards spiral. However, if you manage to take care of things while they're still just small issues you're unhappy with, you can solve them before they become wounds that lead to resentment and defiance. These feelings can be difficult to deal with and can often lead to thinking that divorce is the only option.

These seven paths that you've now read about are all paths that will strengthen your ability to feel intimate with your loved one. When you experience intimacy in a relationship, it opens up the possibility to feel deep love for another human. The more your intimacy is strengthened, the more your love will strengthen.

Good luck to you and your partner in following the 7 Paths to Love.

REVIEW OF THE ADVICE FOR MEN

You mustn't guess what your partner wants, but rather keep asking until you get a clear picture of what your partner's expectations are. If she's unable to answer any of your questions, ask her to think about it. Return to the issue the following evening until you understand her expectations.

Keep in mind that the terms and conditions of a romantic relationship change as we change as humans. It's a good idea to check your relationship yearly so you're certain you're both happy.

You must work on getting better at listening to what you're feeling inside, and use it to get an understanding of your inner compass. This compass is a key element in your relationship. And in other parts of your life.

There are no wrong feelings. Stand by the feelings you aren't proud of as well as the feelings you are. By doing that to yourself, you'll reduce their negative effect magnificently.

Register what you feel like doing or participating in, and clearly say yes to what you want to do. If you don't know what you feel about the suggestion, ask for time to think about it. When you've accepted something or you've agreed upon something, do it without complaining. When you say yes, mean it.

A big potential for your relationship development lies in doing what you aren't used to. Challenge yourself by doing at least one thing you haven't done before with your partner, and register how it makes you feel. Keep what is useful from that experience and throw the rest away.

Find the courage to say no in a proper manner. Stick to what you think even when you are faced with resistance. And remember that sometimes a warm hug can thaw an icy facade.

Focus on your partner every so often, like you do with your hobbies or being with your good friend. When you're being focused on by your loved one, you feel loved.

Use your habit of complaining as a reminder that instead of complaining, you need to do something to make your dreams become a reality.

To get a dignified love life where you can fulfill some of your longings, you need to take responsibility for what you do and the results your actions create.

Decide to get over what happened when it happened, so you can both concentrate on enjoying each other instead of punishing one another.

REVIEW OF THE ADVICE FOR WOMEN

Focus on what you like about your body and ignore the rest.

Decide that you no longer want to worry about yourself and your looks, because a mind without worry stands stronger when faced with challenges.

Use your body to feel how being present and feeling enjoyment is closely connected.

Every time you say that you hate something about your body, you have to mention two things that you love to balance out the negative/positive energy.

Prioritize feeling where your boundaries are and letting your partner know. Clear boundaries create a good environment for the respect among partners. Respect is the basis for intimacy with one's partner in a healthy relationship.

Decide to get to know your own sexuality. And enjoy the wonderful hours you'll have by getting to know your own sexuality better.

The better you get at telling things apart and reacting to exactly what's bothering you, the more you'll increase the chance of intimacy between you and your partner.

Try something you haven't tried before and share your insecurities and vulnerability with your partner while you're exploring what's new. Your man will enjoy being there for you and with you.

You aren't obligated to take on every single responsibility around you. You have the right to prioritize the important and ignore the rest.

Decide that you no longer want to live your love life as if it's a draft of your real life. This is your real love life now, and the sooner you define what you specifically want out of it, the sooner you get to live like that.

Use your habit of complaining as a reminder that instead of complaining, you need to do something to make your dreams become a reality.

To get a dignified love life where you can fulfill some of your longings, you need to take responsibility for what you do and the results your actions create.

Decide to get over what happened when it happened, so you can both concentrate on enjoying each other instead of punishing one another.

One Woman Three Men

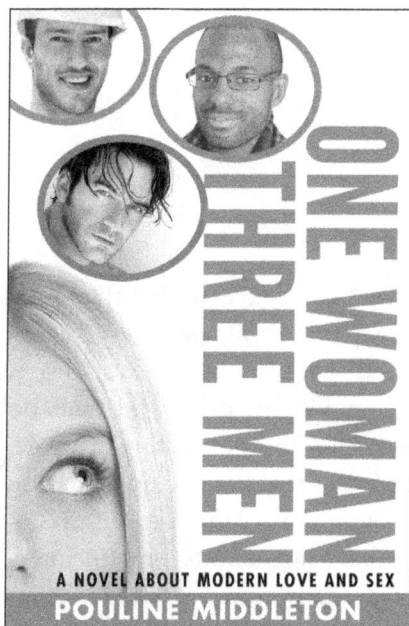

Based on the author's real life story, this is a provocative and intelligent novel about a strong, independent woman (Elizabeth) who decides that the traditional paradigm of dating needs a revolution. Following a divorce and a breakup with a new lover, she decides that trying to get all of her needs fulfilled by a single man just doesn't work in today's world. What she needs is 3 men—one for conversation, one for sex, and one handyman to work around her house. Set in Copenhagen, what follows is a riveting, sexy, saucy tale about her year-long search for three men willing to fulfill those roles—and how this new 1W3M model helped her finally find true love.

Read the first chapter...

APRIL

Dear Diary

'VE BEEN A NICE, well-behaved Danish girl for years, believing that my good behavior would help create peace in 'Palesrael,' equal wages for men and women, and reduced poverty in Africa, while I waltzed into the Copenhagen sunset with my prince, till death do us part. Well, none of this has happened. They're still insisting that war is the way to peace, that women aren't good at negotiating and that's why we don't get equal wages, and that money must continue to flow to support dictatorial regimes even if they have no intention of reducing poverty.

And on a personal level my love life has been blown to pieces yet again, leaving me with no clue as to how to find that prince and move on.

My last love disaster happened right after New Year's . . . Thomas and I were walking on the beach and I was savoring the wind in my hair. He had just flown in from Barcelona where he had gone to sell a painting. I was certain he was on the verge of a big artistic breakthrough. He was painting more and more, using the new oils I had ordered from Milan, and they were helping him with the depth of color and nuances he'd been seeking.

He was not usually one for taking walks as soon as his plane touched ground, but on the way home, he parked at Amager Beach Park right outside the airport, saying he needed to get some fresh ocean air after the stuffy flight. I remember that as we started walking, I slipped my arm into the crook of his, but instead of pulling me closer to him like he usually did, he just kept walking, as if he was trying to get away from me. I reckoned he was tired, and I felt overwhelmed with love for him after what I thought was his grueling three-day trip away.

He was really the best thing that had happened in my life, ever since my divorce from Sebastian, another artistic type whom I was certain I could help. Sebastian and I had met at his band's concert in Berlin when I was 24 and I had been crazy about him. I felt drawn to his intensity both on- and off-stage. He was so sensitive that beautiful music actually raised the hairs on his sexy forearms! When I was seven, I had seen the same thing happen on my father's arms during a Bach organ concert. But while my father is an eccentric though astutely perceptive research scientist, Sebastian turned out to be a rather conventional bass player who spent all his time dreaming about his band's eventual fame, which never happened.

After the divorce, our daughter Mille (age 6 at the time) became my everything. Luckily I only had to be without her every other weekend, which was all that Sebastian could handle of her, the cad. Over time she got used to the arrangement. One morning she looked up at me and said, "Mom, you look tired." I glanced in the mirror, and saw that my kid was better at identifying how I felt than I was.

The next day I enrolled in a Goddess school that my girlfriend Rebecca had been raving about. I wanted to get away from a 'me' I no longer recognized. It took half a year of creating art with emotion, eating unknown foods with all of my senses, soothing my skin with wonderful fabrics from India while listening to other women's stories and sharing mine with them to reconnect with my Goddess self. Little by little, I felt my dreams, wishes and needs rise to the surface again, like a plant that had been submerged in heavy rain lifting itself upwards to the newly reappearing sunshine. Slowly, I regained my pride in being a woman.

Then I dated around for a while, until I met Thomas. He was so refreshing and, well, metrosexual, the first man like that I had ever met. As a struggling artist, he didn't feel threatened by my executive position, and we never fought about money or competed with each other. Mille loved Thomas, too; she even called him Daddy just three weeks after meeting him. The only exception to our smooth relationship were my books, which he felt were everywhere, taking over the house. He pointed this out to me at regular intervals with different levels of frustration in his voice.

Walking there on the beach with him, I was so grateful for our life and the fact that he was so sweet to my girl. But Thomas walked quickly, and I had to make an effort to keep up with him. I felt rushed but didn't pick up on what was coming. He led us toward the pier and turned right. I finally asked if he had had a good trip and managed to sell the painting.

"We need to talk," he said, as he continued walking straight ahead. The thought crossed my mind again that I would have liked to go to Barcelona with him, but Thomas and his French friend Jean-Paul have been going there together every January for years, and I didn't want to break their tradition.

"Something happened in Barcelona," he finally blurted out. He kept walking. "I'm sorry, Elizabeth."

I looked at him. He seldom called me by my full name rather than my nickname, Dixie. My whole body tensed; something was coming.

"I went there with a woman that I've been seeing the last six months. I meant to tell you about it, but it was difficult," he said.

What?!? Then his words, his implication, hit me like a baseball bat from behind. My arm fell from his and I slowed down. He kept walking, saying something I couldn't quite understand. I caught up with him and heard him repeating, "It wasn't supposed to happen like this, but she and I are getting serious, so I have to tell you about it. I'm really sorry."

I walked as if in a trance, my throat tightening. Everything around me seemed to freeze in time and I was unable to do anything to stop it. I blinked in slow motion until I couldn't open my eyes anymore, my tears starting to well up in the corners. The cold wind blew right through my clothing like a sieve. The only thing I could hear was its howl growing louder and louder.

Thomas stared straight ahead and strode directly into the wind as if he needed to get some place. Rage welled up inside me; I seized his arm, trying to make him stop. He tore his arm away, but the force of my grip surprised us both. He stopped and turned away from me. I wanted to scream, but instead I just stood there, glaring at the back of his head.

"She is also an artist," he murmured. "We have a lot in common."

"What do you mean?"

"Well, you know," he said.

"No I don't know," I screamed at him. "You need to come home and paint so you can be ready for a show!"

Tears were now streaming down my cheeks. Suddenly I was 12 years old again. It was early morning and the dim grey Danish winter light my mother

loved was filtering through the windowpanes. I was supposed to be leaving
for school, but if I left, I knew my mother would stay in bed all day and
miss the sunlight that made her so happy. The inner urgency I knew so well
made me set down my bag and enter her room. She was still in bed. Gently,
I pulled her out of bed and helped her get dressed and brought her over
to the studio. She slipped from my arms, landing on the floor with a thud.
I lifted one of the unfinished canvasses that was leaning against the wall,
pointed to a deep cerulean blue and praised her. She stared at me blankly.
I set the painting on her easel and suggested she use it for inspiration, and
then I gave her an encouraging smile for the umpteenth time and left for
school with a knot the size of large melon in my stomach.

When I came home five hours later, I entered the house filled with anxiety and found her sprawled out on the studio floor, holding an empty bottle
of vodka in one hand. The painting was torn to shreds, and she lay with her
head resting on a bit of cerulean blue canvas. The sensation of distress I
knew so well filled me. She was always on the verge of checking out, and I
was convinced it was my responsibility to prevent her from doing it. I raced
over to her and felt her wrist. Her pulse was weak but it was there.

"We need to talk," Thomas insisted again, bringing me back to the present.

My tears kept pouring out. This wasn't the Thomas I knew. My Thomas
loved me more than anything on earth. I've been supportive. I've done
everything I could to help him see life's possibilities instead of its obstacles.
What the hell was he thinking, ruining everything like this? Who was this
woman to make him do something so stupid? And why had he brought her
to Barcelona and not me?

"Come Elizabeth," he said. We were standing next to the car, but I
couldn't remember having walked there. I turned around and started heading back to the beach.

He followed me and shouted, "Come on, we're going home."

"Get out of here!!" I hollered. "You stupid shit!!!"

He ran back to the car, got in and sped out of sight.

I was stunned. I collapsed on the ground where I stood. Thinking about
it now, I remember feeling the coldness of the sand, but I didn't notice it
that day. I sobbed. Without intending to, my mind once again went back
to my mother's studio on one of the many days I found her lying there.

I immediately started to bring her back to bed before father got home, and I barely succeeded. When he asked me where Mom was, I told him that she'd gone to bed with a headache; he was furious and roared that her incessant illnesses had to stop. I sighed and made coffee and whipped cream to serve with cake, and by the time he had eaten, he had calmed down, somewhat. I put Stravinsky's *Le Sacre du Printemps* on the record player for him and went to my room. I believed I was doing the right thing to keep everything from falling apart. Just like I had done with Thomas. I supported, consoled, encouraged, praised and took care of the practicalities so he could make his true potential flourish.

It's been three months now since I last saw Thomas. I've cried and cried, I've talked to my best friends and a number of other people about his infidelity. It really hurt me that he had been seeing another woman for six months. Six months when I thought it was him and me together standing up to the world and then me finding out that I had been all alone. That hurt. I've also talked with people about love to try to understand where it goes wrong. Why in the world is it so difficult?

I'm 34 years old, my daughter lives mostly with me, I love my job helping entrepreneurs become successful, and I long to find a partner that I can have a deep loving relationship with. I want to be part of a relationship where we can both support and challenge each other in becoming our best selves. I want love to be an active partner in my life and not an adversary as has been the case so far. And I'm now prepared to do something different from what I've done before, since that obviously has not worked!

PURCHASE **ONE WOMAN THREE MEN** AT
AMAZON AND YOUR LOCAL BOOKSTORES

ABOUT THE AUTHOR

POULINE MIDDLETON has been a Modern Love coach since 2010. Danish by birth, she holds a M. Sc. in Economics and has worked and traveled extensively around the world, having lived in Paris, Algeria, Hong Kong, and been to 36 states in the US. She worked for several companies in sales and marketing until she decided to become a coach.

Her website is modernloveandsex.com.

We hope you enjoyed this book. If so, please share it with others and write a review on Amazon or other book review websites.

If you are interested in hearing Pouline speak or attending any of her events, workshops or webinars, visit modernloveandsex.com for information about schedules and dates. Workshops include:

THE ONE WOMAN THREE MEN MODEL: Learn how by clearing expectations and defining the areas where you are not prepared to compromise in a relationship you can improve your love life. This workshop will look into the details of one's dreams and expectations of love in order to find the way to a fulfilling love life.

MODERN LOVE: Get an introduction to different models within the concept of Modern Love to find out if any of them appeal to you. The different personal and societal challenges associated with living love in other ways will be discussed.

BOOST YOUR RELATIONSHIP: This workshop will deal with a couple's expectations towards each other. By clearing out some of the 'noise' that exists between partners, couples can identify what kind of life each dreams of living.

You can also contact Pouline at coach@modernloveandsex.com to set up personal coaching sessions.

FOLLOW POULINE:
Twitter: #modernlove, #1W3M, #AskPouline
Facebook: One-Woman-Three-Men
YouTube channel: 1W3M
modernloveandsex.com

www.ingramcontent.com/pod-product-compliance
Lightning Source LLC
Chambersburg PA
CBHW020605030426
42337CB00013B/1214